My Voice OUT LOUD

Inspiring and Soulful Poems about Life, Love, and People

CARYE D. WALKER

My Voice Out Loud: Inspiring and Soulful Poems about Life, Love, and People
by Carye D. Walker

Cover design, editing, book layout, and publishing services by KishKnows, Inc., Richton Park, Illinois, 708-252-DOIT
admin@kishknows.com, www.kishknows.com

ISBN: 978-0-578-66675-4
LCCN: 2020905535

All rights reserved. No part of this book may be reproduced, distributed, or transmitted in any form or by any means, including photocopying, recording, digital scanning, or other electronic or mechanical methods, without the prior written permission of the publisher, except in the case of brief quotations embodied in critical reviews and certain other noncommercial uses permitted by copyright law. For permission requests, please contact Carye D. Walker at:
fivewillcarye32wms@gmail.com
www.poemsbycaryedwalker.com

THE HOLY BIBLE, NEW INTERNATIONAL VERSION®, NIV®
Copyright © 1973, 1978, 1984, 2011 by Biblica, Inc.® Used by permission. All rights reserved worldwide.

Copyright © 2020 by Carye D. Walker
Printed in the United States of America

AUTHOR'S NOTE

*My Voice Out Loud:
Inspiring and Soulful poems
about Life, Love, and People.*

Come with me on a journey that will challenge what we understand about one another. To laugh at one's self is a gift that only we can give to ourselves and each other. Cry with me. Sharing pain or feeling love like no other in a lifetime. Only to lose love. Knowing pain isn't the end, but the beginning of life's book. To know joy in life and to see peace over the horizon even in despair. To feel hope that comes out of pure love of giving. Let me share my story, in words that will inspire and empower us all.

Carye D. Walker

The Wife of Noble Character

A wife of noble character who can find?
She is worth far more than rubies.
Her husband has full confidence in her and lacks nothing of value.
She brings him good, not harm, all the days of her life.
She selects wool and flax and works with eager hands.
She is like the merchant ships, bringing her food from afar.
She gets up while it is still night; she provides food for her family and portions for her female servants.
She considers a field and buys it; out of her earnings she plants a vineyard.
She sets about her work vigorously; her arms are strong for her tasks.
She sees that her trading is profitable, and her lamp does not go out at night.
In her hand she holds the distaff and grasps the spindle with her fingers.
She opens her arms to the poor and extends her hands to the needy.
When it snows, she has no fear for her household; for all of them are clothed in scarlet.

She makes coverings for her bed; she is clothed in fine linen and purple.

Her husband is respected at the city gate, where he takes his seat among the elders of the land.

She makes linen garments and sells them, and supplies the merchants with sashes.

She is clothed with strength and dignity; she can laugh at the days to come.

She speaks with wisdom and faithful instruction is on her tongue.

She watches over the affairs of her household and does not eat the bread of idleness.

Her children arise and call her blessed; her husband also, and he praises her: "Many women do noble things, but you surpass them all."

Charm is deceptive, and beauty is fleeting; but a woman who fears the Lord is to be praised.

Honor her for all that her hands have done, and let her works bring her praise at the city gate.

~***Proverbs 31:10-31 (NIV)***

TABLE OF CONTENTS

POEMS OF INSPIRATION
- Union Pride 3
- A Man 5
- Forever Friend: Larinda's Kin 6
- President Barack Obama: "Man of Hope" 7

POEMS TO EMPOWER
- Her (Blackness) 11
- High 12
- Color Me 13
- Power 14
- Memorable Moments 15
- Kaleena's Touch 16

POEMS FOR CONTEMPLATION
- Black and Blue 18
- My Conscience 19
- Erase Me 20
- Who am I? **Black** 21
- Why Hate? 23

POEMS OF LOSS AND REDEMPTION
- Nightmare 27
- See Glory 28
- Lost Soul 29

- ❃ In Depth and Despair 30
- ❃ Friendship Likened to Fellowship 31

POEMS IN THE KEY OF LOVE

- ❃ Could This Be Love? 35
- ❃ Secrecy 36
- ❃ Embrace Me 37
- ❃ B and T Wedding Call 38
- ❃ Feelings Pour Out 39
- ❃ My Love 40
- ❃ What Is This Thing Called Love? 41

POEMS ABOUT LEAVING A LEGACY

- ❃ Family Honor 45
- ❃ Grandmother's Love 46
- ❃ Big Grand Mommy 47
- ❃ Mom 48
- ❃ Grammy's Girls 49
- ❃ Grandson 50
- ❃ Parent 51

ABOUT THE AUTHOR 53
CONTACT THE AUTHOR 55
PRAISE FOR *MY VOICE OUT LOUD* 57

POEMS OF INSPIRATION

Union Pride

We gather in the hopes to voice out loud,
We carry strong and proud.
All we touch we hold their trust,
To carry on the fight for our rights.
We service throughout these lands,
And foreign plains across the seas.

We embody the cultural diversity
Of our different backgrounds of families.
We continue on a road bound with challenges,
That will bring us ever closer to our goals.
We gather in strength to shout out a roll call…
"Brothers and Sisters" in solidarity.

We humbly embrace our time in leadership roles
With Strength, Sensitivity, Patience, and Consciousness.
Keeping true the values of those we represent,
With educated thoughts and broadminded will from our
Chosen leadership.

We sometimes weep for those we have lost in the struggle,
But we shall carry on this fight with heart and soul.
Organized with traditions that deliver our "cause,"
For we are proud to deliver everywhere, standing tall.

Written for the National Association of Letter Carriers National Convention, to reflect my pride in being a union member and representing my local branch members.

A Man

He is my Son-Brother-Father and Friend.
He walks tall and proud
In the footsteps of his kin.

His spirit is unequal to any other race.
He is judged not only by his intellect but also his skin.

Its race faced to feel out of place,
Daily defeating his opponents, with incredible strength
Within.

He will stand out for the rights of all.
I will be by my Black Man's side for eternity's haul.

Forever Friend: Larinda's Kin

I dreamed of a friend;
To inspire, comfort, defend.
Cherish me
Then uplift and love me.

When I looked up,
You walked in—
Sharing joyful moments
And unimaginable sorrows.

Together, we took a stand,
Uncertain what life plans.
But through it all,
Our friendship endured…
With any dealt hand.

Written for my girlfriend. We were by each other's side through the death of her mom and close aunt from cancer, and then through both of our divorces.

President Barack Obama: "Man of Hope"

The dream came true in our lifetime
To see a Man stand.
That could define a People in pain
That held shame.

No one else could understand
The deep-rooted scars we claim.
A look at first glance of who we are
No other race could comprehend so far.

The intense emotional ride of a separate nation
We have always felt apart.
Today no more the look of power and control
Comes in a new package of a Man.

Self-confident, education-achieved pride of spirits
Raised on shoulders tall for thee.
To believe is "Hope," and to "Hope"
In a life of something better to see.

The good in a country; the United States of America
Truly defined for me.
Finally, a color-blind choice
The world even celebrated with us.

A Man to serve as a voice for human frailty,
And past mistakes politician's boost.
He will carry our country's burden;
A major task that will test him close.

Not one people's choice,
But a melting pot of life's values
And ideas we hold most.
A Man who brings tears of inspiration to my eyes,

That one day, this will be a better day and place
For my children,
As my grandparents and parents wished for their
Offspring and Earth to be.

Barack Obama is that Man
We have all dreamed one day to toast.

Written on November 29, 2008. That was the night that President Barack Obama, First Lady Michelle Obama, and their two little girls, Malia and Sasha Obama, took the stage for the first time as the First Family of the United States of America. I was overwhelmed with emotions of pride and joy.

POEMS TO EMPOWER

Her (Blackness)

Beauty! Behold!
Dark and lovely, we've been told.

Tall, short, big, and small…
Long hair, short hair, bald…we have it all!

Styles come and go; straight, curly, kinky, cornrows,
Weaves…whatever you please.

Never have to look too far,
For our dark beauty
Reflects in and out of us all.

High

Take me high upon your knee,
As a child the wonder I would see.

If I could only reach what would I be,
Flying high like a jet plane ride.

The world wide and full of pride.
Ride high. Fly, baby. Fly!

Daddy's little guy.

Color Me

Black-*Brown*-Coffee-*Mahogany;*
Jet-Black-*Chocolate*-Pepper-*Mocha*-Tan.

Whatever our skin color, it's profound.
Beauty comes in all types and layers bound.

We are all women; beautiful shades of color found.
We are proud to be colorfully crowned.

Power

Strong of mind; knowledge can't be denied.
Mighty is my will, not to be controlled.
I live to succeed another day.
For my blackness comes from the inside.

Pride. Day by day.

We stand upon the backs of our generations call;
That man shall no longer harm us all.
We broke the chains of unrest;
We will no longer fall silent.
Our voices will shout out,

"*Injustice no more!*
 Stop this!"

Memorable Moments

They met, to their delight, in a moment.
It became reality, instead of fantasies' plight.

Life was hard, but driven together they stand;
Through life's ups and downs, in every plan.

Welcomed daughters, who brought them joys grand;
For their triumph forever gave their promises.

Blink of their eye, children grow into women proud.
Motherhood blossomed strong to define their own.

Mom and Dad cherished every moment pleasured;
Giving life lessons with loving treasured.

Wishing all blessings, good health, and cheers;
Many more years of peaceful bliss meres.

Kaleena's Touch

In your eyes…the sun always shines through.
When you smile…the joy surrounds you.

Life has not always been right or perfect for you;
But look at the woman you have matured into.
Stepped out like a butterfly in full bloom.

God blessed the woman who raised you;
As a single parent needs praise too.

The world is a better place because of you;
Your journey still needs to be written by you.

Written for my girlfriend's daughter, who needed to know that she was loved and had accomplished so much without her father in her life. It was to inspire her and other young people that aspire through adversity.

POEMS FOR CONTEMPLATION

Black and Blue

Glazed and cloudy;
The skies open amazed.
Rain for days and days.

It floods and carries me away.

Sadness drags waves;
Wind blows cold prey.
Snow blitzed falls save;

Weather stops. Frozen.

Are we bruised, or do we stand,
And glow throughout this maze?

My Conscience

My eyes were opened to a world of confusion.
My ears heard only diversions.

My head was cloudy with illusions;
My body was riddled with pollution.
Could it be this is all a fantasy?

Or

A world filled with violent tragedies…

Erase Me

Why don't you erase me?
My *heart*
My *soul*
My *body* disappears.

But will it be gone or linger on?

Rhythm of my heart
Listen to hear;
Blood pumping. *Is it clear?*

Who breathes life into tears?
For he has seen inside my fears!

Search for me, if you desire to see;
For no one can just erase me!

Who am I? Black

Lashes across my back, chained from my neck, hands, and feet. What am I? **Black**

Listed as a white man's property and cost less than his animals kept. What am I? **Black**

Sold, hung, raped, and dehumanized as a human being. What am I? **Black**

Fought and won our freedom but still separated by skin. What am I? **Black**

Marches, protesting the rights that others were born with. What am I? **Black**

Woke up to see a day when we are educated, hardworking, and rights achieved. What am I? **Black**

But we still see our rights being sacrificed and dreams broken again. Who am I? **Black**

Killed daily. Jailed often. Lost people. Drugged out streets. Our boys and men haunted by past evils. Who are we? **Black**

We still struggle day and night. Who are we? **Black**

When I go out in the world, I can't hide my skin and face from sight. Who am I? **Black**

Always having to show my intelligence. Not given what I've earned. Double the work and less opportunity. Who am I? **Black**

Who will survive in our communities? Who will stand and be counted?
We the People!

Why Hate?

You say you don't hate, but you lie to the people; propagate.
You call people names and pretend you are their king.
You stir up crazy and play innocent.
You don't know real pain or poor living;
'Cause you're born with silver spoons and gold pots.

You build walls and separate families and children
For praise.
You have no humility or pride.
Just like to boost for sick cheers and face;
You call news fake, but *you* are the phony
Who changes his story at the drop of a hat.
You incite radical behavior and racial divide.
You have no values or moral code of ethics…but we shout!

You are carried by the few…but we will defeat you with
The many.
You will go down in history as a joke,
With tweets for the world to see.
You are a sad and lonely old relic
From past history dates;
Failed destructed thoughts, filled with hate.
It's not too late to save this place from waste.

POEMS OF LOSS AND REDEMPTION

Nightmare

As a child asleep at peace;
A dark touch in the night
To take which was mine.

Causing me a life filled with pain.
My loss of all innocence and blame.
Creating a room closed off; no claim.

Shielding my heart from shame;
Where no one ever knew.
The horror I thought was only mine.

I stood at the crossroads of time—
Looked back at all which was lost; a crime.
I take back all that I buried. Fine!

Let it all go, and free my inner soul's grime.

See Glory

When I open my eyes to a sky of unending stars,
And look at a world of unending scars;
Do I yet cry for all our fears?
Or jump for joy, for our time is near?

Coming for us all; beware but never fear…
When we woke, Oh Heaven had opened His pearly Gates.
For our Father awaits; His children rest.
To nestle in the light of pure grace awaits.

Lost Soul

Oh, my soul feels still incomplete
For who am I, yet to be?
Oh God, please, *please* help me to see…

I'm lost! Can you rescue me?

The pain of life imprisons me.
Goodbye! I am free!
Now can you see…just me?

In Depth and Despair

When I was lost and struggling to breathe…
You gave me air.

When I was hurt and bleeding…
You healed me.

When I had fallen and couldn't get up…
You gave me your hands and lifted me.

When I couldn't see…
You led me.

When I opened my mouth to speak…
You blew life from your lungs to share with me.

When my heart skipped a beat…
You resuscitated me back.

I am here…
Because *you loved me.*

Written the day I was at a low point and didn't know how I was going to pay my bills. My job was in jeopardy. My fellow coworkers rallied and took up a collection. They gave me back my hope.

Friendship Likened to Fellowship

The day I met you, my friend,
It was apparent that there was no forgetting you.
In life's amazing events,
And singular instant moments in time,
My friend came into mine.

You are the one who holds it together,
Even if we all fall apart.
Your calming ability to reach into
Even the most cynical person's thoughts
Is a gift to see.

Inspires us all in our hearts, mind, and soul beneath.
There is no truer friend
Than the one who gives you spiritual awakening
And peace of mind within.
I hope you can see what we have all seen
In you…*glory.*

Through the eyes of someone else
Who has seen you for who you are.
Always a woman who gives herself freely,

With all humility;
And never looks for any glorification
For acts of kindness.

You are blessed for all times…*glory* be
Is through the eyes of someone who sees you
For who you are…
A friend.

POEMS IN THE KEY OF LOVE

Could This Be Love?

Could it be? Love at first sight…
Or was it not until that night?

Could it be? You like me…
Or was it always meant to be?

Could it be? When you held me tight…
Or was it that I felt your delight?

Could it be? Your touch that caressed me…
Or was it your look that possessed me?

Could it be? Those kisses I surrender to…
Or was it that I always knew it to be true?

Could it be? Our passionate embrace…
Or was it the taste you left no trace?

Could it be? The warm feeling that you left me with?
Or was it that we shared a compassion of faith?

Maybe it's just the thoughts we tell our hearts…
My soulmate to face life throughout…

Secrecy

Love; breath sudden and brief;
To touch you, I tremble with disbelief.

Wonder of images my mind has unleashed;
To speak in silence no more, I seek.

My heart cries out softly…*release me.*
Our bodies emerge…*essence of heavenly peace.*

Embrace Me

I feel your arms holding me…*so warm.*
Your touch leaves me helpless.
I melt…*in the heat of your passion.*
That longs for me.
It keeps me…*wanting more.* To be.
My heart…*beats.* Like drums.
Our bodies…*rumble.* Like thunder.

Come to me.

Closer. *Stop.* Wait for me.
Peacefully. *I surrender.* My love.
Our bodies…*explode.* With ecstasy. **"POW"**
You captured me. *All.*

B and J Wedding Call

I take thee…and you accept me.
I see in you the partner
I will build my home and enhance my life.

We both bring from our families
Views…opinions…*attitudes*…
Heartache…*pain*…love…*celebration*…pride.

Neither one of us must lose sight of these.
They are what brought us together
And what will sustain our love for each other
When life struggles seem unbearable.

Because you belong to me, and I belong to you…
This day and tomorrow.

Remember…there is always forever.
Our love, through death do us part.

Feelings Pour Out

In the midst of my window of sorrows,
I see only lost tomorrows.

Like a curtain closed for hours
I shared my heart with yours. It narrows.

We act out the last of our love towers.
The loss of you hits my thoughts. It showers.

Will it be dead in a box? I smell flowers.
Death comes before I find him. It just gets hollow.

My heart feels borrowed.

My Love

I think of you, day and night.

Do you have thoughts of me as well?

Tell me it's not so pale.
If I could reflect on us…
It all fell apart, without any fuss.

It was not meant to be.

You let me go. My heart splits.
Its seams no fix can lift.
I've lost my ultimate gift.

What Is This Thing Called Love?

They said it would be sweet like candy drops.
I disagree.
It has been painful like needles.
Injected through IV-like shots.
I feel lied to. What do they say?

"Love makes the world go round and round."

But my world has been turned upside down,
And round and round,
Like a merry-go-round.
Look closely in the mirror to see;
Love yourself *before*
You can love me.

POEMS ABOUT LEAVING A LEGACY

Family Honor

Traditions are deeply rooted in our ancestry,
For my Grandmother's love
Transcends through family.

She speaks lessons for a life of legacy.
We have discovered substance is the belief that holds our
Family.

Behold our cherished memories!
Even perceives our destiny;
Embrace joy and sorrows of reality.

Our future lies with our offsprings' seed;
To continue the real traditions of this family.
We leave it in their hands, safely entrusted with all deeds.

Grandmother's Love

Grandmother's longevity
Time has frozen.
But her body of enlightenment
Reaches the soul.

Oh! Grandmother knows
Her grandchild's woes.
She peacefully blows
And touches the soul.

But *remember* her weary hands.
With a mother's warmth, wisdom is told.
For the passing of time is our generation's role
Through care and compassion, we learned she left us all.

Big Grand Mommy

I remember so well the love. You gave me care.
Your eyes told your life story of pain;
Those hands and feet showed how hard
You *struggled*.

Worked as a maid, on little gained or earned in aid.
You came from hard stock of man;
Working those Mississippi cotton fields slaved.

Cook, clean, and raise another races children you gave,
While your family suffered with the loss and faded time.

Your strength and heart gave me warmth and
Peace of mind;
If I listen closely, I still hear your voice calling out so
Clear.

Sincere.

I loved you the most. We were so close.
A gift so sweet…rest in peace.

Mom

Made of love for me, God made only one to be.
She was there to wipe away our tears;
And there to give us cheers.

Mom was there to guide us.
When time was tough,
Mom stood tall and defended us.

Her shadow graced our walls.
She was all.
Strength in her hands.
She could do anything.

Her faith gave us encouragement.
Mom showed us true sacrifice;
She's the real Hero to us.

Grammy's Girls

My little princesses are my delight!
They brighten my days and nights!
I look into the innocence of their sights;
My *little angels*. Wondrous spirits. Lights.

Ways to show that their lives will be better
For me, and through them I will see,
A better day for tomorrow.
Innocence from birth. Fresh and new.

My little babies. *Stay true.*
For your life will prosper soon too.

Grandson

You have changed my life with your round face!
So wonderfully bold.
Little body packed up with *so much joy,*
It's gold.

My hope is that your life is what you dream.
Be unique! Break the mold!

Our pride, we hope,
Propels your success into reality goals.
A boy blessed the day he was born,
To be wholly adored.

I *can't wait* to see you grow.
Into a great man's role.

My mighty little soul…

Parent

To feel lost and separate from the world.
A city. A street. A place.
To see my father batter my mom…
He was a beast.

A child's fear that felt isolated and weird.
It was only me and my big brother
With only our tears.

Dad that stole all our childhood innocence and years.
With his own frailty, he covered up his fears
With drugs, crimes, theft, womanizing for years…

Fathering all those kids, I sense a theme;
Threatening to kill us all.
We screamed. This was no dream.

It still haunts me.

Leaving scars that still won't heal.
It got covered up with life's real.
Poor Daddy. All we wanted was your love to feel.

ABOUT THE AUTHOR

Carye D. Walker is a 55-year-old African-American poet who has been writing and turning words into sayings and sayings into poetry since the age of nine. Her love of words has grown through the years.

Carye was born and raised in Chicago, Illinois during the sixties, in the midst of the Civil Rights Era. Although her grandparents and countless aunts, uncles, and cousins helped, times were still hard for her mother, who was raising Carye along with her brothers. They were raised by her strong mother, who taught her and her two brothers that through determination and always believing in yourself, if you never give up, all can be accomplished through faith. Later, her mother remarried, and her stepfather became a defining presence in her life.

Carye grew up feeling that she was different from the other children. She always felt like she had a purpose and needed to be a protector—the one who would stand up for others. She often saw life as fragile and even dark at times; but she always knew that there was more joy in life, if you just look up to the heavens to see the unimaginable beauty in this world. This is what keeps Carye faithful and hopeful. She believes that, "Everyone should take the time to understand what their existence means."

Carye is a passionate, caring person who believes in giving back, and that love will always triumph over hate. She wants to inspire people through her raw words…so that when anyone leaves her presence, they leave wanting more.

Carye has been employed at the United States Postal Service for over thirty years and is a proud Union Steward who has represented hundreds of her colleagues through the years. She resides in Hammond, Indiana and is blessed with two daughters and five grandchildren. Carye hopes that through her poetry, the world would finally understand that it can be a better place and that her grandchildren especially, as well as other children, feel that they are loved and that they belong.

CONTACT THE AUTHOR

Website:

www.poemsbycaryedwalker.com

Facebook:

@MyVoiceOutLoud

@carye.williams.165

Instagram:

@caryed._walker

PayPal:

fivewillcarye32wms@gmail.com

Email:

fivewillcarye32wms@gmail.com

PRAISE FOR
My Voice Out Loud

I enjoyed reading this collection of poems and was impressed that the author shared about her personal life experiences that justify the choices that she made to survive. Her style is rustic, yet it carries a powerful message to engage the reader's attention, inviting them to join her on this journey.

Laying bare her soul and unleashing unbridled passion, she embarks on a journey of self-discovery that teaches love and acceptance, enhances her self-esteem, justifies her existence, and defines her purpose. So she, like the Phoenix, can still rise from the ashes.

From the ashes and pollution of shattered dreams, broken promises, and loss of innocence, she evolves. Her life experiences are chronicled in her poetry, and her use of raw, explosive, colorful language that demands attention lets the reader know that they are in the throes. Through realism and causality, she remains defiantly true to herself, unapologetically *Black,* and undeniably *Woman*. A Mother…with a cause and on a mission.

The caged bird sings; living out loud. She is free! Her faith has sustained her as she stood at the crossroads of uncertain times, when it seemed that life itself had turned on her. With hope, she faces life and whatever it may send her way—a true survivor.

~ MRS. FLORENCE L. DENTON
Retired School Administrator
Chicago, Illinois

I have worked with Carye Walker for nineteen years. During that time, we have had different events and coworkers who have retired. Usually, Carye would prepare a poem for them. The poems would make us laugh and sometimes even cry. When she told me that she had written a book of poetry, I was excited to read it. The first poem I read was special to me because it was written for our letter carriers convention. She spoke on our union values and what they should continue to be.

As I read the rest of the poems, I noticed the variety. There were poems on love, hate, race, and life. While reading the poems, you can feel the passion and emotion that she has put into each one. Each poem leaves you wanting more and ready to dive into the next one. You will not be able to read her poems and not feel anything. After reading the poems, I felt powerful and proud. I have learned that poetry can be therapeutic, and I can't wait to read more of her poetry in the future.

~ CANDICE DELANEY
Letter Carrier
Merrillville, Indiana

My Voice Out Loud. The title of these selections is perfect for Carye. When I read the name of the book, I expected it to be Carye in her raw, sensitive, and passionate self, and I was not disappointed. The poetry selections were full of raw passion.

While reading these poems, you will feel an array of emotions. *Union Pride* really touched home. Having a sense of solidarity in union brotherhood/sisterhood gives you a comforting feeling of belonging. Carye Walker expresses the essence of being a union letter carrier when she stated, "We are proud to deliver everywhere, standing tall." As a letter carrier, you must have pride in the work that you do. You display this by showing up, having integrity, and delivering to hundreds daily.

I felt like my innocence was temporarily placed on hold while reading *Nightmare*. It put me in mind of relatives that have had to live with "a horror I thought was only mine." The horror is not only theirs. There are too many children that are victims of abuse. It brings awareness and informs the abused that you have to "free my inner soul's grime." The poems in this book represent many stages in this game that we call life. We all have been at a point where we felt we couldn't get any lower, like at a financial standstill, or an emotionally high point where you can celebrate a new generation to carry on your family's legacy. She touches on the enlightened feeling of love and being embraced. I knew Carye would publish her poems one day, and I am excited that the world will be able to see and understand her commitment to what she believes in; a touch of struggle, her passion that she exudes daily, and her strength to overcome.

~ *AYESHA S. JONES*
Proud Union Member
Gary, Indiana

Overall, the book was a cool breeze of reality from the author's point of view. The book captivated flashes of life from times that were savory, triumphant, and soberly truthful to all depths and emotions. *Nightmare* reminds the reader to wake up and let go, as the author proclaims, "Let it all go, and free my inner soul's grime." *B & T Wedding Call* reminds newlyweds to keep love in mind at all times, regardless of the good, the bad, and the ugly, and reminding all parties that they are individuals working together to become one. This book will be relatable to all readers, showing the humanity in all life circumstances, perseverance, and beauty. This book will act as a mirror and provide various reflections of life that is relatable personally and connect to real life characters and situations that we all encounter on a daily basis. I enjoyed the author's solidified truth which will speak volumes to the heart space of every reader.

~ Etholia Holmes
Educator, Philanthropist, Youth Advocate
Glenwood, Indiana

Carye Walker's collection of poems is a personal testimony of love, life, and human connection. As you read it, you will take an inspiring journey that feeds the soul. You will experience a wide range of emotions, including pain, sadness, encouragement, hope, and joy. As she reflects on her experiences, you will understand how life evokes emotions.

I was a little skeptical of reading a book of poems since I am not usually a huge fan of poetry. While reading, I found a connection to many of the poems. Each and every poem in this collection has its own meaning. They all share a common purpose that will help you overcome adversity. These words will move you, speak to you, and inspire you as you go through life.

Carye's words offer lessons on encouragement, determination, and faith. They will show you how to garner strength, hope, and love. They will also make you appreciate your loved ones so much more.

~ Dr. Larinda Dixon
Program Chair, Department of Nursing
Professor of Nursing, College of DuPage
Glen Ellyn, Illinois

One can believe that they truly know an individual, especially when an outward appearance reflects a world of calm, steadfastness, and a constant fight to resolve disorder and actions that do not conform to standards of morality. *Union Pride* begins the journey of a voice crying out for justice, and a recognition of being the type of human being that we should all strive to be.

Carye's writings do not recognize a new way to become what we *should already be,* but rather a sorrowful glimpse at what *could have been.* Strong women are prominent in the description of the women she admires; however, sad circumstances appear to continue to repeat themselves. Poems of deep love, abusive partners, and how others see her presents a way of looking at life through the eyes of someone that wants others to hear *My Voice Out Loud.*

The meaning of each writing is straightforward when asking, "Who am I, and why must I continually be judged by the color of my skin, though we come in all shades as black people? God has breathed air into me, and I live because of Him, and though they color me black and *Erase Me,* I'm still here!"

There are feelings of affection and connection, and images of a desire for how things could and should be. The thoughts are wonderful to read, and they bring you closer to a reality that may be part of your own personal life.

I am now closer to an individual that I love and admire as one of my dearest friends. Join me in listening to *My Voice Out Loud* and you too may know that somewhere over the horizon, hope exists and lives inside of you.

~ John E. Spann
NALC President East Chicago, IN 46312
Branch 1399 AFL-CIO

www.ingramcontent.com/pod-product-compliance
Lightning Source LLC
Chambersburg PA
CBHW051411290426
44108CB00015B/2242